W9-BUJ-774

# My First Kwanzaa Book

To Mama, Alma Louise Robinson Newton,
who gave me my first book.
With Love,
DMNC

To my grandson, Jeremy.
With Love,
CM

# My First Kwanzaa Book

By Deborah M. Newton Chocolate
Illustrated by Cal Massey

Cartwheel
·B·O·O·K·S· ™

SCHOLASTIC INC.
New York  Toronto  London  Auckland  Sydney

On the title page: In the spirit of Kwanzaa, art-
ist Cal Massey, using acrylic paints and colored
pencils, has designed a colorful still life linking
the landscape of Africa with elements of an
African-American Kwanzaa celebration. See the
Afterword for an explanation of the symbols of
Kwanzaa.

Text copyright © 1992 by Deborah M. Newton Chocolate.
Illustrations copyright © 1992 by Cal Massey.
All rights reserved. Published by Scholastic Inc., by arrangement
with Just Us Books, Inc., Orange, New Jersey.
CARTWHEEL BOOKS is a trademark of Scholastic Inc.

Library of Congress Cataloging-in-Publication Data
Chocolate, Deborah M. Newton.
    My first Kwanzaa book / by Deborah M. Newton Chocolate: illus-
trated by Cal Massay.
        p.    cm.
    "Cartwheel books" — T.p. verso.
    Summary: Introduces Kwanzaa, the holiday in which Afro-
Americans celebrate their cultural heritage.
    ISBN 0-590-45762-4
    1. Kwanzaa — Juvenile literature. 2. Afro-Americans — Social life
and customs — Juvenile literature. [1. Kwanzaa. 2. Afro-Americans
— Social life and customs.] I. Massey, Cal. ill. II. Title.
GT4403.C464   1992
394.2'68 — dc20                                      92-1200
                                                       CIP
                                                        AC
12 11 10 9 8 7                                          7/9
                Printed in the U.S.A.                    37
        First Scholastic printing, October 1992

# Introduction

Lighting the first candle of the Kwanzaa season is always a big thrill in our household. For seven days, we celebrate the joy of African harvest and culture and the joy of being a family. Each night, by lighting the candles of the kinara, we celebrate Kwanzaa as a holiday of lights.

During the Kwanzaa season, African-American children may wear brightly colored designs that reflect the bold, brilliant textiles rooted in African art and life.

This book is about a boy who celebrates Kwanzaa with his family and learns something valuable about his heritage. The African language of Swahili is used to present the seven cherished principles of the Kwanzaa celebration.

As you learn about and enjoy Kwanzaa with your children, remember that Kwanzaa should be celebrated as a holiday of shared harvest, shared memories, and shared beliefs. My dream is that, one day soon, Kwanzaa will not only be an annual celebration but truly a way of life.

Have a Happy Kwanzaa!

— Debbi Chocolate

When Mama says, "It's Kwanzaa time,"
Daddy helps me dress up in an African shirt.

Mama dresses like an African queen.

December 26
**Umoja**

And Grandma comes visiting with
good things to eat.

December 27
**Kujichagulia**

When Mama says, "It's Kwanzaa time,"
Daddy flies our red, black, and green flag.

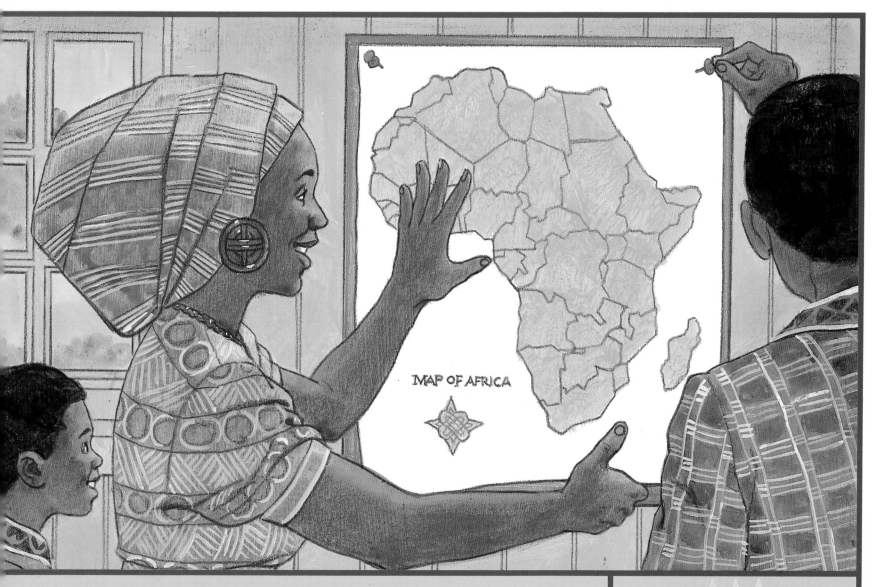

Mama hangs our map of the motherland.

December 28
**Ujima**

And I help light the colorful Kwanzaa candles.

December 29
**Ujamaa**

When Mama says, "It's Kwanzaa time," we tell
family stories each night to make the holiday special.

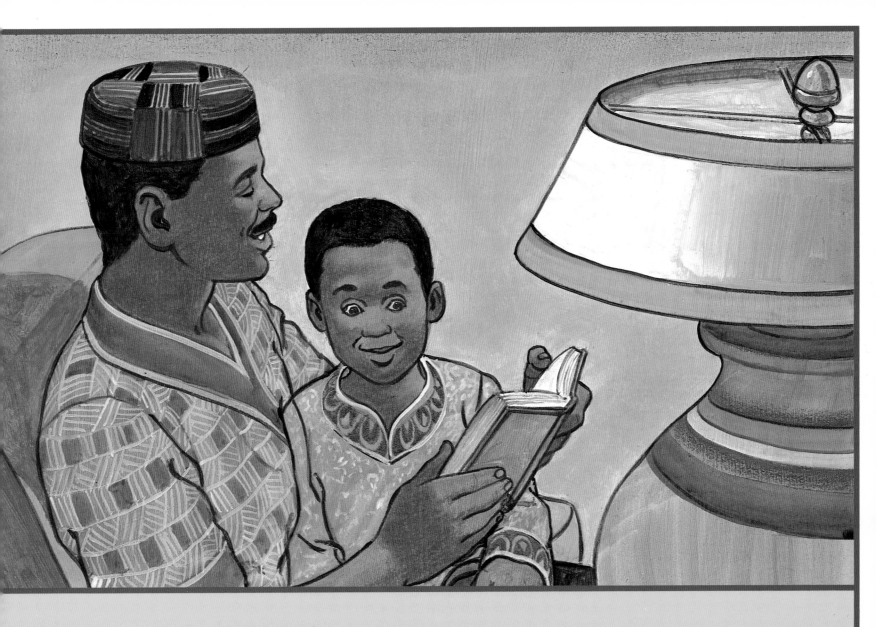

When Mama says, "It's Kwanzaa time,"
Uncle Preedy reads me stories about Africa.

When Mama says, "It's Kwanzaa time," Grandma and I
spend time together stringing African beads.

December 30
**Nia**

When Mama says, "It's Kwanzaa time,"
it's time for a family reunion . . . with aunts from Georgia,

with my uncle from the army,
and with cousins from all over.

December 31
**Kuumba**

And on the last day of Kwanzaa,
we share gifts and hugs . . .

that last until the next Kwanzaa comes.

January 1
**Imani**

# Afterword

The "Father of Kwanzaa" is Maulana Ron Karenga, an African-American scholar and social activist. Kwanzaa was established in 1966 as the only original African-American holiday. Kwanzaa celebrates African harvest and the beliefs and values of traditional African customs. During Kwanzaa, we remember that, while we are Americans, our roots are in Africa, the motherland. The seven principles of Kwanzaa (Nguzo Saba) teach values we should practice every day, not just during the Kwanzaa season.

# NGUZO SABA • The Seven Principles of Kwanzaa

**UMOJA** (oo-MO0jah)
UNITY
We help each other.

**KUJICHAGULIA** (koo-je-cha-goo-LEE-ah)
SELF-DETERMINATION
We decide things for ourselves.

**UJIMA** (oo-JEE-mah)
COLLECTIVE WORK AND RESPONSIBILITY
We work together to make life better.

**UJAMAA** (oo-jah-MAH)
COOPERATIVE ECONOMICS
We build and support our own businesses.

**NIA** (NEE-ah)
PURPOSE
We have a reason for living.

**KUUMBA** (koo-OOM-bah)
CREATIVITY
We use our minds and hands to make things.

**IMANI** (ee-MAH-nee)
FAITH
We believe in ourselves, our ancestors, and
our future.

Explanations for the seven principles have been simplified to help explain them to young children. For detailed explanations, adults should refer to Dr. Karenga's book, *The African American Holiday of Kwanzaa: A Celebration of Family, Community & Culture*. Los Angeles: University of Sankore Press, 1988.

# Symbols and Words Used During Kwanzaa

**bendera ya taifa**    The red, black, and green flag originally used by Marcus Garvey. Red symbolizes the blood of African people and our struggles; black is for the face of African people; and green symbolizes our hopes for the future.

**habari gani**    A Swahili greeting. Loosely translated, it means, "What's new?" or "What's the news?" On each day of Kwanzaa, in the call-and-response tradition of African and African-American cultures, an adult asks, "Habari gani?" A child then replies with the principle of the day, for example, "Umoja!" or "Kujichagulia!"

**harambee**    A Swahili term which means, "Let's all pull together."

**karamu**    A feast that takes place on the sixth night of Kwanzaa, December 31.

**kikombe cha umoja**    The Unity Cup. Everyone who takes part in the Kwanzaa celebration drinks from the Unity Cup to symbolically reinforce the value of unity in the family and the community.

**kinara**    A candle holder (usually of carved wood) with seven candles, which symbolizes the ancestors.

**Kwanzaa**    Kwanzaa is adapted from the Swahili term for "first fruits." Kwanzaa is not a religious holiday.

**mazao**    Fruits and vegetables which symbolize the harvest and the way we work together.

**mishumaa saba**    Candles. There are seven candles: one black, three red, and three green. Each represents a principle of Kwanzaa. One additional candle is lit each day of the celebration — starting with black, then red, then green.

**mkeka**    Mat. The unity mat represents a firm foundation. Mazao and muhindi are placed upon it.

**muhindi**    Corn. The muhindi represents children and their value to the life cycle of the family. One ear of corn is placed on the mkeka to symbolize each child in the household. Children are the center of the Kwanzaa celebration because they represent the hope for the future.

**Nguzo Saba**    The seven principles which embody the value system of Kwanzaa. They are: Umoja, Kujichagulia, Ujima, Ujamaa, Nia, Kuumba, and Imani.

**Pan-Africanism**    A philosophy and practice which affirms the common history, culture, interests, and struggles of African peoples all over the world.

**wahili**   A Pan-African language
poken in at least 13 African countries. It
the language selected for use within
.wanzaa celebrations.

**amshi La Tambiko**   The libation
atement or speech that is made before
ne Unity Cup is passed around.

**amshi La Tutaonana**   The farewell
atement or speech given at the end of
ne Kwanzaa celebration. It is a
eaffirmation of the values of Kwanzaa.

**zawadi**   Gifts. Simple things like books,
heritage objects, or simple handcrafted
items. Zawadi are given to children as
tokens of love and as rewards for work
well done.

## About the Author and Illustrator

### DEBORAH M. NEWTON CHOCOLATE

Deborah M. Newton Chocolate is a writer, storyteller, and educator. She received a bachelor's degree from Spelman College in Atlanta, Georgia, and a master's degree from Brown University n Providence, Rhode Island.

Ms. Chocolate's work has appeared in a number of national magazines and she is the author of the children's book *Kwanzaa*, published by Children's Press.

Ms. Chocolate loves books and children and she enjoys reading aloud to eager, young listeners. She says that writing *My First Kwanzaa Book* was a special experience because it is important to present African-American values to young children n a storybook format. She celebrates Kwanzaa with her husband and two children every year in Chicago where they make their home.

### CAL MASSEY

"I paint because I have to," says Cal Massey. "It's my way of communicating with the world around me."

Mr. Massey is a painter, a sculptor, and an illustrator. He graduated from the Hussian School of Art where he majored in life drawing and illustration. Some of his paintings are in the private collections of a number of distinguished Americans. His works have also been featured in numerous exhibitions and he has created more than 200 designs for medals. Mr. Massey's illustrations have appeared in textbooks, trade books, and magazines. When not painting or illustrating, Mr. Massey applies his artistic touch to baking breads and pastries. He also plays a "mean" jazz piano. Cal Massey and his family make their home in Moorestown, New Jersey.